The Duties and Responsibilities of
the Secretary of
the Treasury

David C. Ruffin

The Rosen Publishing Group's
PowerKids Press™
New York

Dedicated to my brother Bob and to Deborah

Published in 2005 by The Rosen Publishing Group, Inc.
29 East 21st Street, New York, NY 10010

First Edition

Editor: Frances E. Ruffin
Book Design: Albert B. Hanner
Photo Researcher: Sherri Liberman

Photo Credits: Cover (left), p. 8 (bottom) Independence National Historical Park; cover (right), pp. 20 (right), 24 © AP/Wide World Photo; p. 4 © Lee Snider/Corbis; pp. 7, 15, 19 (right) © Hulton/Archive/Getty Images; pp. 8 (top), 11 Library of Congress Prints and Photographs Division; p. 12 (left) © Swim Ink/Corbis; p. 12 (right) © Underwood & Underwood/Corbis; p. 16 (left) © 2004 Gwendolyn Knight Lawrence/Artists Rights Society (ARS), New York. Digital Image © The Museum of Modern Art/Licensed by SCALA/Art Resource, NY; p. 16 (right) Courtesy of Franklin D. Roosevelt Presidential Library; p. 19 (left) Courtesy of the United States Mint. Used with permission; p. 20 (left) U.S. Department of the Treasury, Bureau of Engraving and Printing; p. 29 © Brooks Kraft/Corbis.

Library of Congress Cataloging-in-Publication Data

Ruffin, David C.
The duties and responsibilities of the Secretary of the Treasury / David C. Ruffin.— 1st ed.
    v. cm. — (Your government in action)
Includes bibliographical references and index.
Contents: The Secretary of the Treasury — Money for the American Revolution — The first Secretary of the Treasury — The first income taxes — A system of national banks — A budget for America — Recovering after a depression — The Secretary of the Treasury is not the treasurer — Printing dollars and stamps — The tax man — The job of the Secretary has grown.
ISBN 1-4042-2690-7 (lib. bdg.)
1. United States. Dept. of the Treasury—Juvenile literature. 2. Finance, Public—United States—Juvenile literature. [1. United States. Dept. of the Treasury. Office of the Secretary. 2. United States. Dept. of the Treasury—History.] I. Title.

HJ261.R84 2005
336.73—dc22

                                    2003026342

Manufactured in the United States of America

Contents

The Secretary of the Treasury

The secretary of the treasury is the head of the U.S. Department of the Treasury. This is one of America's most important governmental **agencies**. The secretary is in charge of raising the money that the government uses for all of its programs. For example, without the Treasury Department, the U.S. government would not have money to pay the people who work for its many agencies. The United States would not have money for an army or a navy. The government would not be able to hire scientists for the space program. The secretary also oversees the part of the Treasury Department that prints money and postage stamps. In addition, the Treasury Department has to watch over thousands of banks to make sure they are following banking laws.

◄ *The secretary of the treasury's office is in the U.S. Treasury Building in Washington, D.C.*

Money for the American Revolution

In 1775, the Continental Congress created the Treasurer's Office to raise money to fight the American Revolution against Britain. This was before the United States became a country. In 1788, George Washington was elected the first president of the United States. He had been the commander in chief of the Continental army during the American Revolution. As president, George Washington needed other people to advise him and to help him run the U.S. government. This group of advisers is called the cabinet. In 1789, the U.S. Congress passed a law that created the U.S. Department of the Treasury and the position of secretary of the treasury. Alexander Hamilton became the secretary of the treasury and a member of Washington's cabinet.

Washington is shown here with his 1789 cabinet. From left to right, the people in this engraving are Henry Knox, Thomas Jefferson, Edmond Randolph, Alexander Hamilton, and George Washington.

George Washington signed this document naming Hamilton as the secretary of the treasury.

Alexander Hamilton, ▶ the first secretary of the treasury, worked hard to pay off the money that America owed after the American Revolution.

The First Secretary of the Treasury

President George Washington chose lawyer Alexander Hamilton to be the first secretary of the treasury in 1789 because he knew Hamilton well and trusted his abilities. Hamilton had been Washington's top aide, or assistant, during the American Revolution. Hamilton had been an officer in that war and he had commanded soldiers when he was only 19. He became a member of the Continental Congress when he was 25. Hamilton's first act as secretary was to pay off the money the United States had borrowed. Wealthy Americans and European banks had loaned America money during the war. The money bought the guns, bullets, and cannons that the Continental Congress needed to fight Great Britain. Hamilton also established the first national bank in the United States.

Hamilton established a system for raising money by taxing goods from other countries that came into the United States. These taxes are called customs duties.

The First Income Taxes

In 1861, Salmon Chase became President Abraham Lincoln's secretary of the treasury. Chase had been a U.S. senator before taking the job. The same year Chase became secretary of the treasury, the **Civil War** began. The war was fought between the Northern, or Union, states and the Southern, or Confederate, states over slavery. President Lincoln needed a lot of money to build up a large Union army to win the war. In 1862, Salmon Chase created the **Bureau** of **Internal Revenue**. He convinced Congress to pass the first law to allow the government to collect **income** taxes. These taxes would come from money that citizens and businesses earned. The taxes that Secretary Chase collected helped the Union states to win the war. In 1865, the Confederate states became part of the United States again, and the slaves were freed. Congress removed the income tax law in 1895.

Salmon Chase was a lawyer. He spent much of his career trying to rid America of slavery.

◀ Salmon Chase swears in Abraham Lincoln to the office of president on March 4, 1865.

One of William McAdoo's main jobs as secretary was to find a way to make America's banking system work better.

Through posters like this ▶ one, McAdoo convinced Americans that they should buy bonds to support the war.

"SHALL WE BE MORE TENDER WITH OUR DOLLARS THAN WITH THE LIVES OF OUR SONS?"

W.G. McAdoo
SECRETARY OF THE TREASURY

WE DEPEND ON YOU

BUY A UNITED STATES GOVERNMENT BOND OF THE

2ND LIBERTY LOAN

OF 1917

A System of National Banks

William McAdoo was a lawyer and businessman. When McAdoo became treasury secretary under President Woodrow Wilson in 1913, he faced big problems. America's banks followed many different rules. McAdoo asked Congress to pass the Federal Reserve Act to create a national banking system with one set of rules. He also convinced Congress to pass the Sixteenth Amendment to the U.S. **Constitution**, which made income taxes legal, or lawful, again. This was important because America was spreading westward. The government needed money to build roads and railroads to help the country to grow. The income tax was also necessary for raising money to fight **World War I**. The United States entered the war in 1917, on the side of France and Great Britain. American soldiers fought against Germany, Austria-Hungary, and Turkey. With Secretary McAdoo's financial help, the United States and its allies, or friends, won the war.

13

A Budget for America

Andrew William Mellon, a banker from Pittsburgh, Pennsylvania, came from one of America's richest families. Between 1921 and 1932, he served as secretary of the treasury under three U.S. presidents. They were Warren G. Harding, Calvin Coolidge, and Herbert Hoover. Secretary Mellon began a system to make sure that the government did not spend more money than it possessed. In three years, Mellon cut the costs of running the government in half. He did this by paying the money that the government owed to banks. That way the government did not have to pay **interest** on these **debts**. He also reduced the taxes Americans had to pay. Secretary Mellon's budget was especially successful from 1921 to 1929, when the United States was wealthy. The budget was not as successful after 1929, when the nation's worst **depression**, known as the Great Depression, put millions of Americans out of work.

Andrew William
Mellon is shown at
age 75 in his home
in Pittsburgh,
Pennsylvania.

▲
Mellon was treasury secretary during one of America's toughest times. The
Great Depression left countless people without work. Here men wait in line
to receive food for their families in New York City.

Jacob Lawrence painted this image around 1940 of black people traveling to find work in the North. Lawrence painted during the Harlem Renaissance, when the WPA hired artists as part of its plan to create jobs.

The Tennessee Valley Authority's Norris Dam was built as part of Roosevelt's plan to create jobs.

Recovering After a Depression

Henry Morganthau Jr. was secretary of the treasury under President Franklin Delano Roosevelt. Morganthau was appointed secretary of the treasury in 1934, and he served in that job until 1945. During his years in office, Morganthau helped to create the Works Progress **Administration** (WPA) and the Public Works of Art Project. Both programs gave work to Americans who had lost their jobs during the Depression. He also helped farmers to get loans so that they could keep their farms. When the United States entered **World War II** in 1941, Secretary Morganthau raised about 49 billion dollars to fight the war. This money helped to conquer the countries of **Nazi** Germany and Japan, which had tried to conquer the world.

Henry Morganthau organized the World Bank, which loaned money to European countries that needed rebuilding after World War II.

The Secretary Is Not the Treasurer

The U.S. treasurer works for the secretary of the treasury. He or she has many duties, including receiving tax money and distributing it to different governmental agencies. The treasurer is in charge of producing the coin and paper money that Americans use. Standard coins are produced by the U.S. **Mint**. This bureau makes 14 to 20 billion coins each year. The coins come in amounts from one cent to one dollar. The coins are made at U.S. Mints in Philadelphia, Pennsylvania, and in Denver, Colorado. U.S. Mints in West Point, New York, and in San Francisco, California, produce special coins. Special coins include medals that honor American presidents or special events in American history. These coins are made of precious metals, such as silver, gold, and platinum.

Above are two stages of coin production at a U.S. Mint. Top: Coins are being inspected, or looked over carefully. Bottom: These are newly minted nickels at the end of the production process.

Michael Hillegas was the first U.S. treasurer. He served as treasurer from 1776 to 1789.

◀ Left: *This stamp showing jazz trumpeter Louis Armstrong is one of 10 stamps honoring great jazz musicians. Right: This stamp shows the Grand Canyon in Arizona.*

▲

Bills are being produced at the Bureau of Engraving and Printing. The bureau prints around 37 million notes per day with a total value of nearly $700 million.

Printing Dollars and Stamps

The Bureau of **Engraving** and Printing is part of the U.S. Treasury Department. This bureau produces currency, or paper money. American currency comes in amounts that range from 1- to 100-dollar bills. The money is printed in Washington, D.C., and Fort Worth, Texas. The bureau also prints all postage stamps and hand-engraved invitations from the White House. One concern of the secretary of the treasury's is to make sure that American money is hard to counterfeit, or to copy unlawfully. For example, if you hold a new $20 bill up to a light, you will see a thin strip of words and a picture of President Andrew Jackson that cannot be seen otherwise. These images are hard to copy. Counterfeit money can hurt the American economy.

All paper currency carries the signature, or written name, of the person who is U.S. treasurer at the time that the bills are printed.

The Tax Man

The largest of the Treasury Department's bureaus is the Internal Revenue Service (IRS). Until 1953, it was called the Bureau of Internal Revenue. This is the organization that collects taxes. Taxes provide governmental agencies with money to pay for things that help Americans. Taxes provide money for college **scholarships**, and lunches for students from poor families. Taxes pay for building and maintaining the nation's bridges, roads, and highways. Tax money also goes toward protecting America's national parks. The IRS collects almost two trillion dollars per year, mainly from income taxes paid by American citizens and businesses. Businesses take the taxes out of their workers' paychecks and the money is sent directly to the IRS. By April 15 of every year, Americans will have filled out a 1040 Form, which is a tax report that tells whether they owe money to the government.

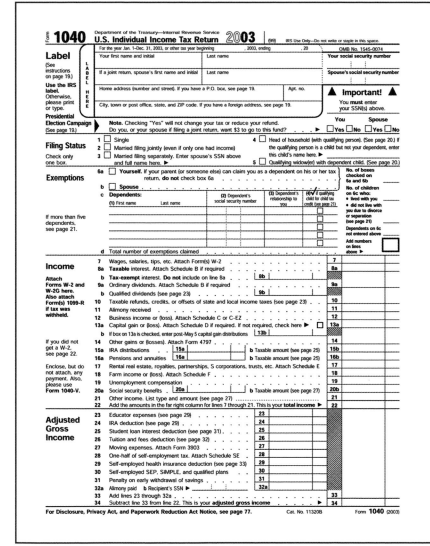

 Each year Americans must file these tax forms by April 15. These forms tell whether a person owes tax money to the government.

Fighting Crime

The U.S. secretary of the treasury also oversees a department called the Executive Office for Terrorist Financing and Financial Crime (EOTF/FC). This office was formed in March 2003 under Secretary John Snow. Its job is to lead the Treasury Department's efforts to fight terrorist financing and other crimes relating to money. A terrorist is a person or group of people that uses violence to force others to do what the terrorists want. The EOTF/FC works with other nations to make sure that terrorists are not able to get money for their plans. The office also works to stop money-related crimes, such as money laundering. Money laundering means that stolen money is made to appear as though it came from a legal source. Activities like money laundering cost the American people and the government a lot of money.

◀ *President Bush looks over the "most wanted" financial flow chart during a tour of the Department of the Treasury's Financial Crimes Enforcement Network in Virginia in 2001. This network became part of the EOTF/FC in 2003.*

The Secretary's Job Has Grown

The Treasury Department has grown during the past 230 years and so have the duties of the secretary of the treasury. In 1775, the secretary of the treasury and a few employees worked in a few rooms in a Philadelphia building. The Treasury Department now has 160,000 employees who work in many buildings, which are located not only in Washington, D.C., but also around the country. The treasury secretary manages the finances of a huge national government. The secretary is also in charge of factories that produce the nation's money and stamps. The secretary has employees who collect trillions of dollars in taxes each year. We depend on the secretary of the treasury and the Treasury Department to keep the United States strong.

The secretary of the treasury has many duties and responsibilities. The thousands of people who assist the secretary work in the agencies of the Treasury Department that are outlined in this chart.

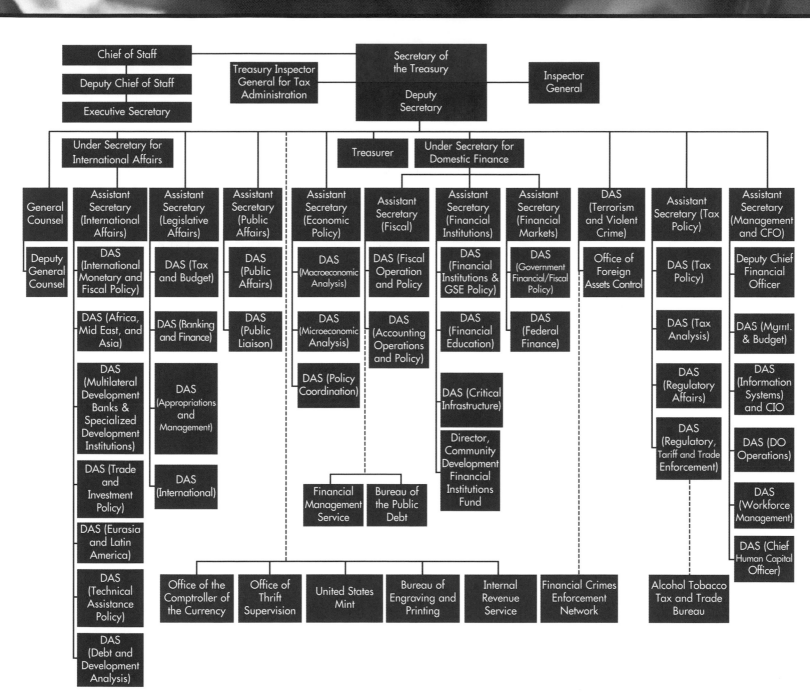

Chief of Staff

Deputy Chief of Staff

Executive Secretary

Treasury Inspector General for Tax Administration

Secretary of the Treasury

Deputy Secretary

Inspector General

Under Secretary for International Affairs

Treasurer

Under Secretary for Domestic Finance

General Counsel

Assistant Secretary (International Affairs)

Assistant Secretary (Legislative Affairs)

Assistant Secretary (Public Affairs)

Assistant Secretary (Economic Policy)

Assistant Secretary (Fiscal)

Assistant Secretary (Financial Institutions)

Assistant Secretary (Financial Markets)

DAS (Terrorism and Violent Crime)

Assistant Secretary (Tax Policy)

Assistant Secretary (Management and CFO)

Deputy General Counsel

DAS (International Monetary and Fiscal Policy)

DAS (Tax and Budget)

DAS (Public Affairs)

DAS (Macroeconomic Analysis)

DAS (Fiscal Operation and Policy)

DAS (Financial Institutions & GSE Policy)

DAS (Government Financial/Fiscal Policy)

Office of Foreign Assets Control

DAS (Tax Policy)

Deputy Chief Financial Officer

DAS (Africa, Mid East, and Asia)

DAS (Banking and Finance)

DAS (Public Liaison)

DAS (Microeconomic Analysis)

DAS (Accounting Operations and Policy)

DAS (Financial Education)

DAS (Federal Finance)

DAS (Tax Analysis)

DAS (Mgmt. & Budget)

DAS (Multilateral Development Banks & Specialized Development Institutions)

DAS (Appropriations and Management)

DAS (Policy Coordination)

DAS (Critical Infrastructure)

DAS (Regulatory Affairs)

DAS (Information Systems) and CIO

DAS (Trade and Investment Policy)

DAS (International)

Director, Community Development Financial Institutions Fund

DAS (Regulatory, Tariff and Trade Enforcement)

DAS (DO Operations)

DAS (Eurasia and Latin America)

Financial Management Service

Bureau of the Public Debt

DAS (Workforce Management)

DAS (Technical Assistance Policy)

DAS (Chief Human Capital Officer)

DAS (Debt and Development Analysis)

Office of the Comptroller of the Currency

Office of Thrift Supervision

United States Mint

Bureau of Engraving and Printing

Internal Revenue Service

Financial Crimes Enforcement Network

Alcohol Tobacco Tax and Trade Bureau

Secretaries of the Treasury from 1789 to 2005

Alexander Hamilton, 1789–1795
Oliver Wolcott Jr., 1795–1800
Samuel Dexter, 1801
Albert Gallatin, 1801–1814
George W. Campbell, 1814
Alexander J. Dallas, 1814–1816
William H. Crawford, 1816–1825
Richard Rush, 1825–1829
Samuel D. Ingham, 1829–1831
Louis McLane, 1831–1833
William J. Duane, 1833
Roger B. Taney, 1833–1834
Levi Woodbury, 1834–1841
Thomas Ewing, 1841
Walter Forward, 1841–1843
John C. Spencer, 1843–1844
George M. Bibb, 1844–1845
Robert J. Walker, 1845–1849
William M. Meredith, 1849–1850
Thomas Corwin, 1850–1853
James Guthrie, 1853–1857
Howell Cobb, 1857–1860
Philip F. Thomas, 1860–1861
John A. Dix, 1861
Salmon P. Chase, 1861–1864

William P. Fessenden, 1864–1865
Hugh McCulloch, 1865–1869
George S. Boutwell, 1869–1873
William A. Richardson, 1873–1874
Benjamin H. Bristow, 1874–1876
Lot M. Morrill, 1876–1877
John Sherman, 1877–1881
William Windom, 1881
Charles J. Folger, 1881–1884
Walter Q. Gresham, 1884
Hugh McCulloch, 1884–1885
Daniel Manning, 1885–1887
Charles S. Fairchild, 1887–1889
William Windom, 1889–1891
Charles Foster, 1891–1893
John G. Carlisle, 1893–1897
Lyman J. Gage, 1897–1902
L. M. Shaw, 1902–1907
George B. Cortelyou, 1907–1909
Franklin MacVeagh, 1909–1913
William McAdoo, 1913–1918
Carter Glass, 1918–1920
David F. Houston, 1920–1921
Andrew William Mellon, 1921–1932
Ogden L. Mills, 1932–1933

William H. Woodin, 1933
Henry Morgenthau, Jr., 1934–1945
Fred M. Vinson, 1945–1946
John W. Snyder, 1946–1953
George M. Humphrey, 1953–1957
Robert B. Anderson, 1957–1961
C. Douglas Dillon, 1961–1965
Henry H. Fowler, 1965–1968
Joseph W. Barr, 1968–1969
David M. Kennedy, 1969–1971
John B. Connally, 1971–1972
George P. Shultz, 1972–1974

William E. Simon, 1974–1977
W. Michael Blumenthal, 1977–1979
G. William Miller, 1979–1981
Donald T. Regan, 1981–1985
James A. Baker, III, 1985–1988
Nicholas F. Brady, 1988–1993
Lloyd M. Bentsen, 1993–1994
Robert E. Rubin, 1995–1999
Lawrence H. Summers, 1999–2001
Paul H. O'Neill, 2001–2002
John W. Snow, 2003–Present

◀ *Secretary of the Treasury, John W. Snow*

Timeline

1775	The Continental Congress creates the Treasurer's Office to raise money to fight the American Revolution.
1789	The U.S. Congress passes a law to create the U.S. Department of the Treasury. President George Washington names Alexander Hamilton the first secretary of the treasury.
1791	The Bank of the United States is established.
1861	Upon becoming the tenth U.S. treasurer, Frances Skinner upset many people by vowing to hire women at the Department of the Treasury.
1862	Paper currency is first printed in the basement of the Treasury Building.
1913	Congress passes the Sixteenth Amendment to the U.S. Constitution, making income taxes legal and permanent.
1921	Secretary of the Treasury Andrew Mellon creates a system to make sure that the government does not spend more money than it possesses.
1941	A War Finance Division is created to have Americans buy and save savings bonds to help pay for World War II.
1949	President Harry S. Truman names Georgia Neese Clark to be the twenty-eighth treasurer and the first woman to serve in that office.
1957	The term "In God We Trust" is first printed on all U.S. currency.
2003	EOTF/FC is formed under Secretary John Snow.

Glossary

administration (ad-MIH-nih-stray-shun) A group of people who direct an organization or company.

agencies (AY-jen-seez) Special departments in the government.

bureau (BYUR-oh) An office or department.

Civil War (SIH-vul WOR) The war fought between the Northern and the Southern states of America from 1861 to 1865.

constitution (kon-stih-TOO-shun) The basic rules by which the United States is governed.

debts (DETS) Something owed.

depression (dih-PREH-shun) A period during which business activities are very slow and many people are out of work.

engraving (en-GRAYV-ing) A design or picture that is cut into wood, stone, metal, or glass plates for printing.

income (IN-kum) Money received for work.

interest (IN-trest) The extra cost that someone pays in order to borrow money.

internal revenue (in-TER-nul REH-veh-noo) Taxes that the government collects from businesses and citizens.

mint (MINT) A place where a country's official money is made.

Nazi (NOT-see) Referring to a German political party, or official party, under the leadership of Adolf Hitler.

scholarships (SKAH-ler-ships) Money given to someone to pay for school.

World War I (WURLD WOR WUN) The war fought between the Allies and the Central Powers from 1914 to 1918.

World War II (WURLD WOR TOO) The war fought by the United States, Great Britain, France, and the Soviet Union against Germany, Japan, and Italy from 1939 to 1945.

Index

Web Sites

Due to the changing nature of Internet links, PowerKids Press has developed an online list of Web Sites related to the subject of this book. This site is updated regularly. Please use this link to access the list: www.powerkidslinks.com/yga/drst/